Samuel Miller Hageman

The Divine Malignity

As Opposed to the Divine Paternity

Samuel Miller Hageman

The Divine Malignity
As Opposed to the Divine Paternity

ISBN/EAN: 9783337779801

Printed in Europe, USA, Canada, Australia, Japan

Cover: Foto ©Lupo / pixelio.de

More available books at **www.hansebooks.com**

THE DIVINE MALIGNITY

AS OPPOSED TO

THE DIVINE PATERNITY

BY

S. MILLER HAGEMAN

PRINCETON, N. J.

———————

NEW YORK

TROW'S PRINTING AND BOOKBINDING CO.

201-213 EAST TWELFTH STREET

1885

Dedicated

TO

CALVIN BURNING SERVETUS

EXASPERATED BY

AUGUSTINE, TERTULLIAN, EDWARDS,

THE SUPERIORS OF

THE DOCTRINE OF THE DIVINE MALIGNITY,

OR,

VINDICATORY JUSTICE, A PRIMORDIAL TRAIT OF GOD

Presented to

THE NINETEENTH CENTURY CLUB

OF

NEW YORK

THROUGH

Mrs. COURTLAND PALMER

CONTEXTUAL EXCERPTS.

FOR this does not consume what it burneth, but repaireth what it preys upon, so that the mountains which always burn remain, and this may be a Testimony of that Eternal Fire, which continually nourisheth and preserveth those that are punished by it. — *Tertullian.*

Many more are left under the vengeance of God than are made objects of His saving grace. — *Augustine.*

The whole world does not belong to the Creator. Grace delivers a few who would otherwise perish, but leaves the world in the destruction to which it has been destined. — *Calvin.*

The two worlds of happiness and misery will be in full view of each other. The saints in glory will see how the damned are tormented. A sense of the opposite misery greatly increases the relish of any joy or pleasure. Every time they look upon the damned it will give them a more lively relish of their own happiness; it will be an occasion of rejoicing as it will be a glorious manifestation of the glory of God; therefore the damned and their misery, their sufferings and the wrath of God poured out upon them, will be an occasion of joy to them. They will be hated with a perfect hatred. God never loved them and never will love them.
— *Edwards.*

From age to age the elect have been very few. They make only a little flock, which almost escapes our notice. — *Massillon.*

Little children and young infants, though they live but a minute, are in as great danger as men that live a hundred years. It is not for your time that God will judge you, but for the odious nature of sin. — *Christopher Love.*

Little child if you go to Hell there will be a devil at your side to strike you. Neither father, nor mother, nor brother, nor sister, nor friend will ever come to cry with you. The same law which is for others is also for children. See a terrible sight. The little child is in this red hot oven. Hear how it screams to come out. See how it turns and twists itself

7

about in the fire. You can see on the face of this little child what you see on the faces of all in Hell—despair, desperate and horrible! At this moment a child is going into Hell. To-morrow evening go and knock at the gates of Hell and ask what the child is doing; the devils will go and look. Then they will come back and say : "The child is burning." Go forever, and forever you will always get the same answer, "it is burning." Children will be frightened there. Do you know what is meant by being frightened out of one's senses? A boy wanted to frighten two other little boys. In the day time he took phosphorus and marked the form of a skeleton on the wall of the room where the little boys always slept. In the day time the mark of phosphorus was not seen, in the dark it shines like fire. The two little boys went to bed knowing nothing about it. Next morning they found one boy sitting on his bed staring at the wall, out of his senses. The other little boy was dead. That was fright.—*Father Furnis' Tracts for Little Children for the year 1881, published permissu superiorum, representing the doctrine of the Roman Catholic Church and acknowledged as such by the authoritative allowal of its publication.*

Nay one could go farther, and could hold that contrast may be a necessary factor in the Divine economy, and that for aught we know the Eternity of Evil finds some explanation here.*—*Professor Patton in Princeton Review for 1878.*

Human punishment unlike the Divine is variable and inexact, because it is to a considerable extent reformatory and protective. The Divine Tribunal in the last great day is invariably and exactly just, because it is neither reformatory nor protective. And this work is to satisfy justice. The human penalty that approaches nearest to the Divine is capital punishment. The reformatory element is wanting.—*Dr. Shedd, North American Review for 1885, pp. 160-9.*

The goodness, yea the exceeding mercy of God in creating human beings who he fore-knew from all eternity to be eternally damned.—*Lyman Ashland. Sermons for 1885.*

I started suddenly, there was a voice beside me, a young woman with a babe on her arm.—*Letters from Hell, 1885.*

---

* In other words if we define the fatalistic chiaroscuro of Necessary Contrast with which this writer sums up this whole theological diabolism it stands squarely thus : " What were Heaven in all its splendor without Hell to set it off."—Tнᴇ Aᴜᴛнᴏʀ.

He who rids the world forever of a superstition
   base,
Is the greatest benefactor, dead or living, of
   his race.

S. MILLER HAGEMAN.

In its sleep, bent o'er a City, weeps a figure
carved to Pity,
Through whose eyes and lips and fingers runs
an old heart-broken rhyme :
And the throngs that lean and listen as those
trickling tear-drops glisten,
Little think themselves are pictured and the
thoughtless Lapse of Time,
Sounding down its way sublime,
With its many-fountained music and its mul-
titudinous chime.
Oozing, trickling, bubbling, gleaming,
Laughing, weeping, sobbing, streaming,
Wailing, murmuring, sighing, dreaming,
Flowing, flowing on.

11

So stand we, that dreaming sleeper, as the
shades of life grow deeper,
And the Lapse of Time is flowing through the
fountain of our years:
Seconds, minutes, hours, hasting, through our
heart-throbs, wasting, wasting,
Trickling through our hands forever into grasp-
less hopes and fears,
    Till at last Time disappears
Down the dimly-lighted valley, down the val-
ley of our tears.
  Tinkling, plashing, rippling, creeping,
  Bounding, sparkling, dancing, leaping,
  Foaming, billowing. tumbling, sweeping,
    Gliding, gliding on.

12

Time--thy shadowy stream emerges from its
    thousand-folded surges,
Where, as sunlight dreams to moonlight, mem-
    ory and mystery meet:
On whose oriency welling, slowly widening
    cycles swelling.
Round the wild fantastic echos, so fantasti-
    cally sweet,
        That the river doth repeat,
To the music and the motion of its fluctuating
    feet,
    Welling, dripping, pattering, plashing,
    Spouting, roaring, booming, dashing,
    Volleying, avalanching, crashing,
        Moving, moving on.

Through the pillared grotto's brimming, twink-
ling little boats go skimming,
Down the deep perspective dimming, slowly
down its marble hall;
And faint peals of song and laughter, "Vale,"
"Vale," sound long after,
Down that dim Æolian river they have van-
ished at our call,
As the echoes float and fall.
Echoes of departing souls, as Night and Silence
wraps them all.
Echo's, echo's, echo's flying,
Up and down the river dying,
Still repeating, still replying,
Flying, dying on.

14

Deep through darkened cavern gliding, deeper
    still within it hiding,
Save the small white fishes sliding eyelessly all
    to and fro;
Loud and louder sounds the splashing of the
    waters, dashing, dashing,
As some blundering rock goes crashing down-
    ward with the torrent's flow,
        With reverberating blow,
Down, down, down, the echoing chasm, down a
    hundred feet below.
        Echo's, echo's, echo's meeting,
        Up and down the river fleeting,
        Still replying, still repeating,
        Sounding, sounding on.

15

On it flows by dell and dingle, where the
  drowsy flock-bells jingle,
Tink a tank a tingle, lingle, as the sheep wind
  slowly home:
On by day with flowers a-winkle, on by night
  with stars a-twinkle,
Drowsing, dreaming, richly creaming all its
  banks with flowery foam,
    As its waters onward roam,
On with baa-aa and noo-oo—and tinkle, as the
  herds clang slowly home,
    Through the corn and through the clover,
    Through the rock-beds, under, over,
    So Time goes, a restless rover,
      Roaming, roaming on.

Through the palms the golden pheasant glitters
    like a yellow crescent.
To the crocodile's low chuckle all along its
    leafy chinks:
As from out the stifling rushes some tall ibis
    loudly brushes,
Whips the blue air with his white wings, flies
    off—till at last it sinks,
        Down upon some sun-red sphinx,
Tired of standing—doubled up—on one leg by
    the reedy brinks,
        And a cangia down the river,
        On whose oars the moonbeams shiver.
        Swift as arrow from a quiver
            Shoots and flashes on.

On that undulating river, hurrying phantoms
sway and shiver,
Never lifted veils of Isis, but Time lulls them
with its lay:
Knocks at hut and throne and castle, calls alike
to king and vassal,
Calls, as age and youth and childhood with its
willowy waters play,
Calls, and as they turn to stay,
Whispers to them, "Come" and washes,
washes all their feet away.
Idling, basking, loitering, purling,
Eddying, quirking, darting, whirling,
Sporting, chasing, rushing, swirling,
Drowsing, drowsing on.

18

Down it drops through layers of peoples, down
    through crypts and courts and steeples,
Bares a brow, a loin, a sceptre, and a throne
    with monarch set:
Captain-jewelled-crowned Osiris, circled with
    the magic iris,
All, as once they looked on Egypt, still on
    Egypt looking yet,
        Face to face in silhouette,
Ranked along that runic river, mirroring all
    Time ever met.
      Cangias, jewels, crystals, vases,
      Orgies, odors, voices, faces,
      Tear-drops, passions, torn embraces,
        Drifting, drifting on.

Down it rolls and down it rages, thundering
from out the ages,
Down a deep, volcanic whirlpool, pouring with
its frenzied throng;
Through an old Pompëian city, crying, "Jesu,
Nunc Dimmitte."
O'er whose shipwrecked crew Time's river omi-
nously flows along.
Listen, as it flows along,
To the revelry, to the devilry of that cacopho-
nian song.
For it seems all sounds intoning,
Wheezing, muttering, cursing, groaning,
Hooting, howling, bellowing, moaning,
Moaning, moaning on.

Brightly stands that human torrent, shudder-
ing back as if abhorrent,
Sunset of lost souls all going down in darkness
and in doubt:
Tantalus, with wild endeavor, drinks the watery
drought forever,
Round whose Thirst-cup whorls the whirlpool,
round its heterogeneous rout,
Round and round its hollow spout,
Round and round and round forever, but it
cannot wash it out.
In its coil a serpent couches,
Open-mouthed it cranes, it crouches,
Sucks—and with distended pouches,
Sucks—and swallows on.

21

Through its dim mysterious portal on whose
crest a mythic mortal *
Strains a silver cloud forever to his cheated
bosom fond;
Through its shadowy recesses that its labyrinth
confesses,
Deep from out that inky darkness a diaphanous
creature dawned,
That forever did respond,
"Come with me and I will light you through
this labyrinth beyond."
She, with singing and with smiling,
She, with languoring face, beguiling,
All her pits with victims piling,
Many a soul lures on.

* Ixion embracing Juno.

I had seen in marbles scented, in old tapestries, tormented

Contours of this curious creature at whose feet the snake's mouth yawned;

Wrought of woven wind the vapory tissue of whose trailing drapery,

Whispered on the cheequered marble with its lanceolated frond,

As her heavy eyes despond.

Standing there a yellow leopardess in the tamarisk shade beyond,

Far from love and virtue straying,

Far from home and wrung hands praying,

Dice and drink and music playing,

She, her web weaves on.

E'en the while I did behold her, from the clasp
upon her shoulder,
Slowly slid the purple peplum till about her
feet it fell:
And beneath the round pilaster, like a lamp in
alabaster,
So her soul shone through her body, as a sea-
nymph through its shell,
So she sang her syren-spell,
Luring foolish mortals downward till their
feet take hold on hell.
"Come," she sighed with cruel malice,
"Come," she sighed with cup and chalice,
"Come, with me into my Palace,"
"Come with me, come on.

21

* Oms ! what means thy growling thunder, why
thy pent, thy wild-eyed wonder?
See ! the gates of Hell are opening and a soul
goes in a-train :
Howls of rage and yells of laughter, ringing
back from roof and rafter,
Swell the wild tremendous uproar of each gong-
resounding chain,
  Rend the Book of souls in twain.
And a name—your name upon it and the gates
crash too again.
 Be it god or demon muttering,
 Be it fiend or fairy fluttering,
 Round it rustling shapes are cluttering,
  As that soul glides on.

   * Oms, the Dog of Hell.

Swift from out the crimson flurry clutching
    griffons hiss and hurry,
Beaked and talon-hooked together, fiends of
    every sort and size;
For a share of her damnation, piece-mealing
    with delectation,
One by one each shape that enters in her train
    with fiery eyes;
      Ghoul-watched gate of Paradise,
Verminous with griffons craning at each shadow
    as it flies:
      Satyr, gorgon, dragon, goggling,
      Scorpion, vampire, bogie, boggling,
      Harpy, pixy, ogre, oggling,
        Gloating, gloating on.

* O'er its arch that deadly sentence, *once within
it—no repentance,*

Every face a branding horror, every breath a
smoking prayer,

Burning floors and vaults and dresses, burning
chains and wings and tresses,

Burning hands flung up for torches that but
light them to despair,

Swirling down that headlong stair.

Swirling, bottomlessly swirling, down, down,
down that dizzy stair.

In each drop I seem discerning

Countenances dazzled, turning,

Sizzling, crackling, blistering, burning,

Burning, burning on.

* All ye who enter here leave hope behind.

Swart amid them sits the devil on a throne in
ghastly revel,

Rattling in his monstrous shackles all the prison-
house of Hell:

One hand pointing light supernal, and the other
gloom infernal,

As he cries, " For God a handful, but for me
these myriads tell,"

    " All these peopled planets tell,"

" All these starry camp-fires burning in the bi-
vouac of Hell,"

  Sun and sky and space enshrouding,

  Threatening, gathering, blackening, clouding,

  Rumbling, thundering, piling, crowding,

    Crowding, crowding on.

"All are called but few are chosen," warm
    Heaven in a tear-drop frozen,
Thinly sown the path to glory, but devoured
    the road to night:
Here and there a hermit's taper shines, elect,
    through mantling vapor,
'Mid the windows that are darkened in the
    Palace of the Light,
      Darkened Palace of the Light.
Till a grand deserted ruin Heaven stands out
    against our sight.
      Nearly all God's throne forsaken,
      Nearly all God's crown outshaken,
      And its captain-jewels taken,
        Satan has it on.

There the vast assembled millions, tiered on
    billions, tiered on trillions,
Lost long years before the coming of that Christ
    they ne'er should see:
There that fog-like army rising from the sea,
    a satirizing
Swarm, and all without a Saviour, damned and
    damned eternally.
        Think of it—eternally,
All past Time a point forever to the Timeless-
    ness to be.
    And the distant " Ever " " Ever,"
    Echoing back the " Never " " Never,"
    Runs through Acheron forever,
        On and on and on.

There the troops of little winning sinners ere
  they knew of sinning,
Lost for but a drop of water, sob along those
  walls a-side;
Too deformed for recognition, masked the bet-
  ter for derision,
Till the spirit of St. Vitus would be fully sat-
  isfied;
    Father, mother, sweetheart, bride,
Through the glare of dazzling darkness diabol-
  ically eyed
  Countenances, knotted, staring,
  Leering, mocking, taunting, glaring,
  Scowling, glowering, wild, despairing,
    Dead but living on.

31

There the gowks. the dwarfs, the dragons, idiots
    straining fiery flagons,
Shrivelled wails. sleep-walking shrouds, gnarled,
    bleared enormities a-file :
There, uncouched, the sick, the weary, deaf
    and dumb and blind and dreary,
Moralist and Magdelena flung to one incestuous
    pile,
      Lifting up high Mass the while,
Typhon writhing under Ætna with its mon-
    strous ebony smile.
      Tangled stack of serpents, coiling,
      Hissing, fanging, frothing, boiling,
      Tightning, festering. weltering, toiling,
      Writhing. writhing on.

Burnt in Effigy God's creatures, with his stamp
    upon their features,
Gorgon smiling back Apollo, carved to monu-
    mental man;
All that image fast departing, on those stony
    eyeballs starting,
Hands o'er hands of blackened pillars holding
    up Heaven's gorgeous span,
        Sport-making Sampsonion!
Bow thyself—thy unshorn fury would pull
    down the eternal plan.
      Towering up a human Babel,
      Reaching Heaven, out-fabling fable,
      And yet but a stony table
        Law is writing on.

Down upon that city burning, looks the face of
   God discerning
Everything in Heaven turning red with its
   reflection set :
Blood-shot moon upon Gibraltar, as upon its
   smoking altar,
Flames the smile of satisfaction with its relish-
   ing regret
      O'er Heaven's red-robed parapet,
On death-kissed remembered faces, and yet able
   to forget.
      Two worlds turned toward one another,
      Two souls in them, child and mother,
      One in Heaven—in Hell the other,
         Smiling, sobbing on.

Look down through the gates below thee,
   mother, on those eyes that know thee,
Can'st thou say from Heaven's "Good Morning"
   to that child Hell's "Good Night!" No,
Can'st thou from that orphan ever turn and
   say " Our Father !" Never.
By a mother's love I cannot, will not, dare not
   make it so.
      She had left Heaven long ago,
Crying out—" If this be Heaven then to all
   Hell will I go."
   Be she saint or be she sinner,
   While that child cries out within her
   " Mother," 'twere not God to win her
      While that child cries on.

Not a star above but nightly for the darkness
    shines more brightly,
What were Heaven in all its splendor without
    Hell to set it off?
What were light without its shadow on the
    cloudless Eldorado?
What were joy without its sorrow, what were
    song without its scoff?
            Each to set the other off,
And a gluttony for glory and a skeleton at its
    trough,
        Till in turn no less amazing,
        Lurid Hell on Heaven lies blazing.
        See! the angels with their glazing,
        Bloodshot eyes look on.

What are all those people burning in that
   whirlpool redly turning?
Burning Joss-sticks to Jehovah seated on the
   throne of Thor:
He who, like that king of glory in an old bar
   baric story,
When the enemy had landed burned their ships
   upon the shore,
      That they should depart no more,
Wrapt asbestos-like in fire yet unconsumed,
   that siege ne'er o'er.
      Writhing in a wild endeavor
      To appease God's wrath, ah never,
      Great Implacable! forever,
         Love sits hating on.

37

"I will laugh at their disaster. I will mock
as fear comes faster.

"I will sit as a refiner bringing out what sin
begat:

"I will sear the shining lenses of their filmy-
folded senses,

"Lest, mayhap, they be converted, till the
fire drops out thereat,

From the wine-light of the vat,

"Mercy, when I will have mercy," think'st
thou ever God said that?

Laughing—while fresh vengeance waking,
Laughing—while a world forsaking,
Laughing—while his heart is breaking,
Laughing, laughing on.

Are they all alike forsaken, is the last, the last
    kiss taken?
Suffering for the sake of suffering, a revenge
    that mortals spurn:
Thus, as virtue God condoning what his creat-
    ures are disowning,
That as Time's slow-fingered Sybil book by
    book its volumes burn
        In the ashes of their urn,
There shall still be always something left of
    sin for sin to learn.
    Still the Sybil sits there turning,
    All that lore of guilty learning,
    And though leaf by leaf is burning,
        Still a leaf turns on.

But suppose them thus deserted, and the Face
  of God averted,
What free choice in such a creature without
  God—yet God begot?
Without eyes, damned for not seeing; without
  feet, damned for not fleeing;
Without ears, damned for not hearing; without
  wills, for choosing not,
        Judgment over—Justice—What?
Down in such a spiderous dungeon immortality
  would rot.
        All in Thee, Thou great All-seeing,
        All in Thee, thy shadows fleeing,
        Live and move and have their being.
        Dead in Thee—live on.

Shut a child up in a closet, till the stifling
   darkness awes it:
Hear its sob, " O Mamma, mamma," dwindle to
   a moan, a sigh :
Go some morning and undo it; look, O mon-
   ster, look into it,
See! a little heap of ashes, all that's left of
   that bright eye,
      And the whole world cries out, Fie!
Yet you leave that very closet on God's hands
   eternally.
      You do more—you turn its story
      To a shamble grim and gory,
      In which God, for his own glory,
         Stands and slaughters on.

Sin—you punish—yet preserve it—steal Heaven's fire with which to serve it,
Fan it till a wild contagion leaps through corridor and hall :
Till the cyclone hath arisen, till the lightning strikes the prison,
Slam the lid down on the caldron, "Come out " to the chained wretch call.
That is Hell—if that appall,
To preserve sin and forever were the greatest sin of all.
Guilt that makes high God its miser,
Hoarding up with vault and visor,
Dark Malignity grown wiser,
As its plot goes on.

42

Thou who all our hands hast broken from the
hands that wave no token,
Does forgiveness turn to hatred in a single hour
above?
Eye that warms not, weeps not—answer—in
thy breast that burning cancer,
Says, "for this there now is nothing, nothing
left that Love can do."
"Nothing left for God to do."
"But to sit and smile and feel it burning, burn-
ing through and through,"
Spoken to, but never speaking,
Sought, alas, but never seeking,
God have mercy—but that reeking,
Eye looks on, looks on.

Still o'er all that burning city, weeps that figure
    carved to Pity,
With the water trickling, trickling, through its
    eyes and hands and lips:
Still that terrible clepsydra, through its human-
    headed hydra,
On each brow in molten minutes maddeningly
    drips and drips,
      And a spectre sips and sips,
And a rainbow playing in it over all that wild
    eclipse.
    Peeping through their dungeon-grating,
    Peeping, calling, crouching, waiting,
    Beckoning, listening, watching, waiting,
      Vainly, vainly on.

And those spectres will be found there, when a
  cycle shall go round there,
At those bolted doors of Doom with charred
  heads listening at the grate
For a knock—that falleth never, though they
  wait for it forever.
Key and keeper gone to glory, and the prison
  locked—Too late!
        O Thou Irony of Fate!
With thy hand--a shaking palsy—fumbling
  for a latchless gate.
    Hopeless—yet forever hoping,
    Bandaged-swathed, yet blindly groping
    Toward those doors that shut in ope'ing,
        Shut and open on.

Dost thou still refuse to reason? then to sleep
   to-night were treason,
Fie thee on this earth, O preacher, till thou all
   that horror tell:
Stop the clock, for Time is over, stay the scythe
   a-cut the clover
Hang the houses all in mourning, drape the
   plough, the wheel, the bell
      Toll the deep-toned funeral knell,
For the village, for the city, for the whole
   world is in Hell.
   Why, since Hell you hold my brother,
   Why, with holy water smother?
   Paint it as you paint the other,
      All its colors on.

46

All its groans, its pants, its embers, all its love
    no love remembers,
All its human-heaving contours, all its fever-
    crimsoning face,
All its tears, its scars, its blisters—and that
    smile on Heaven that glisters,
All, for God's eternal glory, all to show abound-
    ing grace;
        All for glory, all for grace.
Better Christ had died on Christmas than such
    glory, than such grace.
      God for judge and Heaven for jury,
      Did the world believe that. surely,
      It would be a slinging fury
        Ere an hour rolled on.

Lost—a foundling—at Heaven's portal, born
dead, but a dead Immortal:
Lost—a child—without a mother; lost—it
knows not where or how:
Lost—a soul—without a warning, sun eclipsed
at gates of morning:
Lost—a ship—without a captain, but his
shadow at the prow;
    Lost—but none so lost as Thou.
Lost unto Thyself, yet on Thyself all intro-
verted now.
    Like a longforgotten story,
    Like a song of lark or lory,
    Lost—in light of thy own glory,
      Adnate-faced, lost on.

What hath this God-pointing slander done to
    make the great world grander?
Hath it glorified religion, frightened nations
    with its fume?
It hath filled the earth with scorners standing
    upon all its corners,
It hath made Christ's death a failure, it hath
    wrapt the world with gloom,
        In the shadow of its doom,
Till each word we speak sounds ghastly as a
    death-groan from a tomb.
      It hath taught the church to palter,
      It hath taught the heart to falter,
      And to stand still at the altar,
        While the lips moved on.

I begod a God supernal working out a good
eternal,
But a God who let Time's chain down link by
link into the grave :
Saw the end from the beginning, made a world,
and with it, sinning
Creatures that he could not govern, creatures
that he could not save,
Offered pardon to a slave,
To a soul he felt beforehand doomed and
damned ere life he gave;
Diabolical! the Devil,
In his wildest rage and revel,
Never touched so low a level,
As such God stands on.

All the types of human passion that the brutal
    ages fashion,
All the gods of mythic fury meet in such a
    God above.
Wouldst thou coin a splendid casting of that
    One God everlasting?
All his attributes are written in those three
    words, " God is Love."
     Grand, exhaustless Godlike Love;
There it stands—the one solution of the world's
    great problem—Love.
      Not in wrath vindicatory,
      Not in nature's starry story,
      This is God's eternal glory,
        Loving. loving on.

Thou, of this great ball the moulder, charged
    with it against thy shoulder,
Thou, that sweepest the horizon, Thou so sphere-
    less, we so small:
Thou hast made us—by that token, can the
    bond 'twixt us be broken?
Thou hast made us. Shall thy image from its
    shining pedestal
        Into darkened ruins fall?
Thine we are. Thou hast no orphans. Thou
    the Father of us all!
    Who hath need of such a blessing,
    Who hath case so wildly pressing,
    As a wretch, thy love transgressing,
    Still transgressing on?

Nothing dies—the distant "Ever" is the echo
      of the "Never,"
Silence is but unheard music sounding some-
      where still in space :
Somewhere in the distance dying, bugles calling,
      colors flying,
Troy is carrying off Helen, Cain strikes Abel in
      the face.
            Veiled in melancholy lace,
In some cloud-bower Eloisa falls in Abelard's
      embrace.
            And the "Ever" and the "Ever,"
            To the "Never" and the "Never,"
            Through the river runs forever—
            And forever on.

Bring me up the blackest Ethiop stooping down
    to drink all Lethe up,
In that fiend a bright Celestial gleams out of
    his eyes again :
Still for him all sweet sounds tingle through
    his memory as they mingle,
Still for him a bird is singing, and a flower
    tincts all the glen,
      Something in him now as then,
'Tis the far-off " Alter Ego " Time is bringing
    out in men.
      For, if holiness eternal,
      Lost St. Satan once supernal,
      Why should sin hold him infernal,
        As that sin goes on ?

O infallible Tradition, crossed with priestly
    superstition—
I and God—Imperial It—the thing done tells
    God what to do :
God saw not what Galileo saw, knew not great
    Kepler's " Deo,"
Nor the fall of Newton's apple, though by that
    same apple too,
      Adam fell and downward drew
By its law of gravitation, sin you never did on
    you.
      All the suns and stars that dapple
      This vast Universe, shall grapple
      With the theft of that one apple,
        Falling, falling on.

He who rids the world's sad story of a super-
stition hoary,
Is the greatest Benefactor, dead or living, men
confess :
He who shows the world its Vision, shall hold
up to high Elysian,
The eternity of evil—that great curse—the
churches bless,
To be nothing more nor less,
Than a grand apotheosis to stupendous nothing-
ness.
After smiling, after weeping,
After sowing, after reaping,
Nothing left but love worth keeping,
Ever, ever on.

When God's hand the World had moulded
  slowly through long time unfolded,
Last to come and late to ripen, in his lowest
  form came man :
Man shall sin, and, sorrow-laden, ere he finds
  that sorrow's Aäiden,
Stand for all his solemn shadow far beyond
  where he began ;
          But beyond this earthly span,
Man shall be a higher being, built upon a higher
  plan.
          Patience is God's pastime, slowly
          He is lifting up the lowly,
          To the pure, the high, the holy,
              Upward, upward on.

Still o'er all that burning City, weeps that fig-
ure, pale with pity,
From whose eyes and lips and fingers Time in
blood-drops trickles through :
And the throngs still lean and harken as the
shadows round it darken :—
Such a sin and such a Saviour as its deep ver-
milion drew,
At the Cross that City threw.
Father ! Father ! O forgive them, for they
know not what they do !
O ye priests, ye schools, go borrow
Justice, from that dying sorrow !
Yesterday, to-day, to-morrow,
Jesus Christ ! live on !

Jesus Christ! divinely human—something man
   and something woman,
Crown of universal empire claims no other king
   but Thee:
From the deserts Ethiopic, from the ocean and
   the tropic,
From the glittering suns and systems that go
   round Immensity,
      (For they all belong to Thee)
" I, if I be lifted up will draw the whole world
   unto me."
      Hark! I hear—a whispered thunder,
      Filling all the world with wonder,
      'Tis the tread of millions under
         Coming, coming on.

For, did Christ, though God's hand beckoned,
   with anxiety unreckoned,
See down through the gates infernal one whom
   once he loved so well:
He would turn his back on glory, on its song
   and on its story,
Tear the crown from off his forehead, and the
   robe that round him fell,
      Hurry down to darkest hell,
Crying, "Judas." "The Lord's Supper"—that
   is irresistible.
      That is Christ—sublime engraving,
      Holy with its human craving,
   Souls worth making are worth saving,
      While a soul throbs on.

I behold their lighted tapers, rising from the
  whirlpool's vapors,
Through the crescent pales of being up the
  steep of world's afar:
I behold them—the Past hovers—the air throbs,
  the eye discovers
Up vast flights of steps—a Throne-Cross—
  shining in a nightless star,
    Two Thieves at its Judgment bar.
"To bless Heaven is good," the judge says, " to
  bless Hell is better far."
    Rags and shame and destitution,
    Vice and squalor and pollution,
    All that wails for absolution,
      Bless that—bless, bless on.

Flow, thou stream of Time, flow coldly, and
through all that City boldly,
With thy waters wash it, wash it, all away
forevermore:
Earth grows still, its voices mumble, ships and
cities rot and crumble,
Skeletons of nations whiten to the wild beasts
famished roar,
  Sinks its last sun low and lower,
Life is dead—the world deserted—darkness
falls—and Time is o'er.
  Dimly earth's last soul descrying,
  Faster and still faster flying,
  In the golden distance dying,
    Dying—dying—gone.

www.ingramcontent.com/pod-product-compliance
Lightning Source LLC
Chambersburg PA
CBHW030854260626
47169CB00008B/2532